Searching
for
Nova Albion

ALSO BY PAMELA CRANSTON

Poetry

Coming to Treeline: Adirondack Poems

Nonfiction

An Eccentric English Journey (Limited Edition)
Clergy Wellness and Mutual Ministry
Love Was His Meaning: An Introduction to Julian of Norwich
A Spiritual Journey with John Donne

Fiction

The Madonna Murders

Searching for Nova Albion

Poems by
PAMELA CRANSTON

RESOURCE *Publications* • Eugene, Oregon

SEARCHING FOR NOVA ALBION

Copyright © 2019 Pamela Cranston. All rights reserved. Except for brief quotations in critical publications or reviews, no part of this book may be reproduced in any manner without prior written permission from the publisher. Write: Permissions, Wipf and Stock Publishers, 199 W. 8th Ave., Suite 3, Eugene, OR 97401.

Resource Publications
An Imprint of Wipf and Stock Publishers
199 W. 8th Ave., Suite 3
Eugene, OR 97401

www.wipfandstock.com

PAPERBACK ISBN: 978-1-5326-8419-7
HARDCOVER ISBN: 978-1-5326-8420-3
EBOOK ISBN: 978-1-5326-8421-0

Manufactured in the U.S.A.   JUNE 18, 2019

For the Rev. Zoila Schoenbrun
and
Redwoods Monastery

> "We shall not cease from exploration
> And the end of all our exploring
> Will be to arrive where we started
> And know the place for the first time."

—T.S. Eliot, from "Little Gidding V," *Four Quartets*

> "God, of your goodness give me yourself, for you are sufficient for me. I cannot properly ask anything less, to be worthy of you. If I were to ask less, I should always be in want. In you alone do I have all."

—Julian of Norwich, *Revelations of Divine Love*, VI

Contents

Permissions / xi

Acknowledgments / xiii

I / 1

By Porth Neigwl Bay / 3
Walking in Muir Woods / 5
Searching for Nova Albion / 7
The Weaver / 9
Sand Dollars at Sandy Hook / 10
Why Redwoods Grow So Tall / 12
The Timber Reapers / 14
Labyrinth in Sibley Park / 15
The Green Gulch Dragon Bell / 17
Honeysuckle in Havertown / 18
I Am the Rosebush, I Cry / 20
Chances Are / 21
Firestorm / 23
Wedding Poem / 25
Seeing Daniel Berrigan for the First Time / 27
Diptych for David / 28
The Factory of Making / 30
Sowing Seed / 31
Van Gogh's Sower with the Setting Sun / 32
The Double Opening / 34
Carriers of Strange Fire / 36

II / 39

And Isaiah Said / 41
Shaker Chair / 43
Rosebush in Early Summer / 44

Always Autumn / 45
A Priestly Prayer / 47
The Golden String / 48
The Watchers / 50
For Some Death Comes / 51
What If the World Was Wider / 52
Duino Revisited / 54
The Kerastion / 55
Why Thanksgiving Day Will Never Be the Same / 56
The Promised Land / 58
Magnolia Blues / 59
Prayer of the Hermit Crab / 60

III / 61

The Fountain and the Tower / 63
Distilling the Core / 66
Palm Sunday 1212 / 67
The Keeper of Julian's Shrine / 69
Gleaning for Gooseberries / 71
Compline / 72
A Troubadour Romance / 73
To Our Lady of the Redwoods / 75
Elegy for a Monk / 76
An Unexpected Visit / 78
Jacob at Peniel / 80
The Tent of Meeting / 82
When Roses Bore Berries / 83
A Poem for the Feast of Christ the King / 86
Advent / 87
Zechariah's Annunciation / 88
The Language of Angels / 90
Soundings / 92

IV / 95

Songs of the Logos / 97
   1. The Turning Word / 97
   2. God's Annunciation / 98
   3. The Midnight Day Star / 99
   4. Gauguin's Mary / 100
   5. The Baptism / 102
   6. Christ in the Wilderness / 103
   7. God, What a Wind / 104
   8. The Teachable Moment / 105
   9. The Transfiguration / 107
   10. The Passion Tree / 108
   11. Resurrection / 109
   12. The Stone of Grief / 110
   13. Emmaus / 112
   14. The Ascension / 114

Notes / 115

Author Biography / 117

PERMISSIONS

My thanks to the editors of the following journals and publications in which poems from this book have previously appeared, some in different form:

Anglican Theological Review: "And Isaiah Said," "Always Autumn," "Searching for Nova Albion," "By Porth Neigwl Bay," "The Double Opening," "Shaker Chair," "I Am the Rosebush, I Cry," "Gleaning for Gooseberries," "God's Annunciation," "Zechariah's Annunciation"

The Anglican Journal: "Poem for the Feast of Christ the King"

Christianity and Literature: "Palm Sunday 1212"

Edgz: "The Kerastion," "Why Redwoods Grow So Tall"

Women Healing and Empowering: "Resurrection"

The Golden String: Journal of Dom Bede Griffiths Trust: "The Golden String"

The New Moon Review: "The Green Gulch Dragon Bell"

A New Song: "Emmaus"

Pacific Church News: "Rosebush in Early Summer"

The Penwood Review: "What If the World Was Wider," "Van Gogh's Sower with the Setting Sun"

Excerpt from "Little Gidding" from *Four Quartets* by T.S. Eliot. Copyright © 1942 by T.S. Eliot, renewed 1970 by Esme Valerie Eliot. Reprinted by permission of Houghton Mifflin Harcourt. All rights reserved.

Forty-three (43) words from REVELATIONS OF DIVINE LOVE by Julian of Norwich, translated by Clifton Wolters (Penguin Classics, 1973). Translation copyright © Clifton Wolters, 1973.

Albert Einstein quote in "Chances Are," from *What Every Principal Would Like to Say . . . and What to Say Next Time: Quotations for Leading, Learning,*

PERMISSIONS

and Living by Noah benShea. Copyright © 2000, Corwin: A Sage Publications Company, p. 94.

Simone Weil quote in "The Double Opening," from *Waiting for God* by Simone Weil, translated by Emma Craufurd. © 1973, Harper & Row, New York, p. 166.

William Blake quote in "The Watchers," from *Jerusalem. The Emanation of the Giant Albion*, Chapter I/Plate 77 by William Blake, written and etched 1804–1820. Source: *Complete Poetry and Prose of William Blake*, Newly Revised Edition. Edited by David V. Erdman. Commentary by Harold Bloom. Copyright © 1982, University of California Press, p. 231.

Thomas Traherne quote in "What If the World Was Wider," from *Centuries of Meditations* by Thomas Traherne, edited by Bertram Dobell. Bertram Dobell Publisher, 1908. p. 12.

Kierkegaard quote in "The Promised Land," from *Seekers: Finding Our Way Home* by Paul Dunion. Copyright © 2006, Archway, p. 15.

Charles Wesley quote in "Jacob at Peniel," from *Watching Over One Another in Love: Reclaiming the Wesley Rule of Life for the Church's Mission* by Michael G. Cartwright and Andrew Kinsey, Copyright © 2011, Wipf and Stock, p. 23.

Scripture quoted by permission. All Scripture quotations are taken from the Holy Bible, New English Translation, NET Bible™. Copyright ©1996–2016 by Biblical Studies. All rights reserved.

Cover art: *New Albion: Sir Francis Drake's Ship Golden Hind* (canvas, oil) by Simon Kojin. Copyright © 2008 by Simon Kojin. Reprinted by permission of Simon Kojin. All rights reserved.

ACKNOWLEDGMENTS

The author is grateful to the following people for reading these poems over many years and for their continual support and encouragement: Nicoli Bailey, the Rev. Dr. L. William Countryman, the Rev. Connie Hartquist Jacobs, and the Rev. Zoila Schoenbrun.

I am especially indebted to my editor, Suzanne Underwood Rhodes, for her skill at wielding her pruning knife with diligence, tact, understanding, and a keen poet's ear.

Finally, none of this would be possible without the humor, constant support, and abiding love of my husband, Edward Cranston.

I

BY PORTH NEIGWL BAY

(For R.S. Thomas: 1913-2000)

We drive down the long green spine
of the Llŷn Peninsula,
past hard-bitten towns
with soft names—smooth
as melon in the mouth, names
like Mynytho and Rhiw
and unpronounceable Pwllheli.

Your whitewashed cottage,
clabbered as curds,
perches on the lip
of Porth Neigwl Bay
above a spare shingle of beach
where the tide
cracks its knuckles all day.

Fishermen call this tiny Welsh cove
"Hell's Mouth"—an ironic place
for a poet-priest unable to utter a bad word.
Legend says a lost village lies beneath the bay.
When the wind and waves are right,
you can hear muffled bells
throbbing in the sunken spire.

I suspect you came to soak
in the aged stillness,
to hear silence ripened by the rise
of ancient prayer, to catch
the hidden chimes ringing in the wind,
licking your heart's cold metal
into song.

Maybe you hoped to hear them
toll the changes,
even as your own soul finally
learned how to undress itself

and put on (for once)
the sweet cloak
of absence.

WALKING IN MUIR WOODS

I'm here
to sit at the feet
of giant sages who stand
like wizards
with their rusty wooden cloaks
wrapped about them.

I think their essential work
is to lift all things—
to extend their arms up
in high exultation
and carry this wounded world.

Who knows, maybe
their soaring prayers,
dusky as incense,
even buttress highest heaven?

Silence is their truest language.
This has taken me a lifetime to learn.
From my seat on a mossy log,
I watch and wait not knowing
what wisdom they will teach.

And then, like a sign,
a snowy egret flutters down,
a handkerchief dropped
by an angel, a page
of God's stationery, a hymn
composed by the wind.

It wades into the water on stilts,
a Tai Chi Master
taking each slow step.
It stretches and cranes its snaky neck,
like a seer with piercing eye
probing the heart of things.

This is how a poet
should walk on the earth.

SEARCHING FOR NOVA ALBION

All my life I've been westering.
Today I'm on pilgrimage
to Drakes Bay. I drive past
bookstores, theaters, and boutiques,
past remnant groves of redwoods
rapt in contemplation,
past oyster beds bubbling by Tomales Bay,
and farms, gray as driftwood
splintered by the muscling mist,
to the farthest curb
of this California coast.

Drakes Bay lies fourteen miles out:
shafts of sunlight wash
the white-curdled cliffs
leaving yellow softness.
I blink my eyes
to glimpse how Drake
saw the untouched sand.

Surely he saw the same greedy gulls,
their craws bulging with perch;
the kelp in clumps
like brown tangled mops,
the lonesome pelican bobbing on the waves—
the calligraphy of sandpiper tracks,
and walls of green glass rising
in the sea's silent elevator,
brimming toward thunder.

Except back then this beach
thronged with countless birds,
unharmed by slicks of sludge.

Let me be clear.
I am not like Francis Drake,
that ruthless pirate-explorer
ever flashing his prized pearl pendant.

I'm more like Chaplain Fletcher,
earnest, principled, and bookish,
clutching his prayer book,
wondering how to speak
against Tom Doughty's death
and praying for dry land,
as one would for rain.

I tend to seek safe passage
wherever I go.

But who can stand to see power abused
or the stripping of Albion's beauty?
Who is willing to be the last
to hear a curlew sing?

Maybe this poem is my first small sword.

Sir Francis Drake charged his co-commander, Thomas Doughty, with mutiny and treason, and had him beheaded on July 2, 1578. On June 17, 1579, Drake landed his ship, the Golden Hind, in what is now Drakes Bay on the Point Reyes peninsula in California, for repairs. A day or two after, the ship's Anglican chaplain, the Rev. Francis Fletcher, celebrated the first Book of Common Prayer communion service in North America, with the captain and crew in thanksgiving to God for landing safely. Drake named the region Nova Albion [New Britain] and claimed it for the English crown. When the ship ran aground on a reef in Celebes in January 1580, Chaplain Fletcher preached a sermon calling the captain and crew to repent, suggesting that the near wreck was divine retribution for the murder of Tom Doughty. When they finally set sail, Drake struck Fletcher with his slipper, chained the clergyman to a hatch cover, and ex-communicated him[1].

THE WEAVER

The trading post was crowded—
cluttered with kitsch and restless chatter.
Tourists dug coins from their pockets like pay dirt
buying Mars bars and postcards,
Navaho beads and blankets.

Nearby, an old man with silver braids
sat quietly at his loom.
He bent to the rhythm of his work
like a willow wooing lake water.

Deftly, he slipped the wooden shuttle
through the woolen weft—
a slender fish he caught
and let go,
then caught again.

I sat with my back against the wall
and watched. His patience lifted the room
into a reaching forest, filling the air
freely as water flows
around unforgiving rocks.

As the warp and woof of his loom shut,
clicked open then shut again,
it seemed his weaving healed
a hole in our needy world.

Sometimes you come across a person
so still,
it pulls you out
of your lonesomeness.

SAND DOLLARS AT SANDY HOOK

(For Nicoli Bailey)

Below Agate Gap
a stony spit of land
digs into the gill of Puget Sound
like a fishhook.

Out of work and counting dimes,
I spend myself on freer things.

I'm a child of Mt. Marcy
and other Adirondack matrons,
so I know little
about seaside ways. Little

about green tresses of seaweed
splayed upon static rocks,
about the litter of busted shells
or the sharp tenacity of barnacles,

about carrot-colored stones
thumbed smooth by the tidal hand,
crab carcasses tossed ashore
like rusty tin cans,

conch shells lying like ears
open to the Sound's endless sighing—
the antiphonal rumble and whoosh
of waves breaking on the sand.

Especially the delicate sand dollar.
The first I've ever found!
Most lie crushed and broken,
but some are perfect

white moons
etched with the five-petaled lotus
risen from the bottom
of their murky horizons.

At sunset, I stroll home,
lighter and richer,
with ten full moons
floating in my pocket.

WHY REDWOODS GROW SO TALL

Watch a coastal redwood
long enough, you'll catch it
listening. It rises so high,
at first you think it star-pulled,
winched from outer space—
solitary, detached from the cares
of lowly earthworms and sparrow cries.

But no redwood ever grows alone.

Look with eyes closed and see
how wide its root-thrust extends.
Not from a single taproot,
but from an intricate, buried web
of sturdy thatch.
Redwoods march together,
a family of giants
with arms linked together,
sharing their stories.

And not just with each other
but with raven and deer,
cougar and salmon, with dragonfly
and inchworm—even stories
of you and me. Together
our storylines climb the rings
rising up the core, and carve
a thousand trenches
in weathered bark.

A redwood grows wise
by attending to its neighbors,
then takes each story
and offers it
with upstretched hands.

It has done this so long,
its fingers
touch the fringe of heaven.

THE TIMBER REAPERS

In the middle of a tree-rimmed field
stands a tall incense cedar
stretching two pinnacles
into the air—prongs

of a tuning fork, humming
harmonies to heaven.
Butterflies winnow
the air in obeisance.

Over the ridge crest
a buzz saw growls
and whines as it slices
the torso of a tree.

From this far, I hear the crash
before I feel the ground move.
Did the cedar also feel
the felling of its neighbor?

Two foresters in overalls
are thinning the woods.
Today, they won't harm
the grand cedar, but someday

someone will, for greed
or (at least) for tidiness' sake—
when one more high-pitched
silver tong will cease its ringing.

LABYRINTH IN SIBLEY PARK

Slipping away to repair
the tatters of my day,
I climb down a quarry
in a snuffed-out volcano.
Green shoulders slope
like the downs of Dorset.

I've come to hear the wind
whisper its insistent song,
to see a goshawk
scissoring the air in flight.

Below a ledge, I find
a winding circle of stones,
a newly hatched maze
erupting from the brown skin
of mothering earth.

Barren stones, almost prehistoric,
describe the circle of life—
an ancient Womb of Being.

Beside them, a marsh
of red-winged blackbirds
perched on cattail spears
screech and bob in the wind.

Skeptical, shuddering
from the strangeness,
I refuse to step inside the circle,
decline to walk
the rocky path of pilgrimage.

Safer to stand
on the lip of the labyrinth
and imagine its call,
trusting it traces a trail
to the core
of my own locked heart.

I know what the stones are saying:

*Don't be afraid
to travel the darkening way.*

*The journey in
always takes much longer
than the journey out.*

*All you need
is to begin.*

THE GREEN GULCH DRAGON BELL

(For the Green Gulch Farm Zen Center)

Imagine if a Samurai warrior
dressed in silver armor
suddenly clambered down these cliffs
strewn with poppies and gorse,
and stopped to kneel in silent prayer
then froze in place.

The Green Gulch temple bell
rises each morning like that warrior,
a fierce priest, its voice breaking
out of its metal cloak, to sound
a stern gong of summons, rousting
the monks from sleep's sweet cradle
to gather in silent praise.

And don't all of us wake up,
no matter where we lie—
by mountains or cities or farms,
needing that hammer-call
to shake us out of our ruts
and blind attachment
to attachment.

Each day the trick hand of chance
gives us a choice—
to grow through suffering,
or not at all.

Listen to the lesson
of the green dragon bell:
safety is the surest means
to turn your heart to stone.

HONEYSUCKLE IN HAVERTOWN

We lived on a corner lot
in a white Cape Cod cottage
tight as a Shaker hutch. A patch
of green grass, a short path
linked me to the outside world
and best of all, the playground.

Some days, I had nothing to do
but study how tenacious weeds
(always invincible) drilled holes
through the gray concrete,
which sloughed white dust
and stank in the summer heat
like condensed shale.

One morning, plunging into a rush
of cool air glazed with honey,
I puzzled the source of it
till my nose led me
to a waterfall of honeysuckle
spilling over a chain-link fence.

This toppled gold was revelation.
If it was honey cake,
I would have eaten it—
if nectar, drunk it.

I envied the bumblebee,
yellow and plump as a school bus,
how it buzzed all day,
diligent in its work, dipping
its furry body again and again
down those pink throats of plenty.

If only I could drench myself
inside that breast of bliss!
If only I had gossamer wings!
Each morning, I'd float away
all dusted in sweetness.

Each morning, I'd know
what vocation was.

I AM THE ROSEBUSH, I CRY

Half a rosebush high
I toddle
with tender feet
to where the gardener
has manure-tilled
the salmon roses sweet.

I am the rosebush, I cry.
I am the honey red.
I am the earth, the trees, and sky.
I am my sleepy bed.

The lazy bees and I
we hum
a humble tune.
I know how the roses know
my face this afternoon.

I am the rosebush, I cry
I am the honey red.
I am the earth, the trees, and sky.
I am my sleepy bed.

When Grandma calls
I come
crawling like a lamb
from my place
of straw and thorns
to the dawning of I am.

CHANCES ARE

"Coincidences are God's way of remaining anonymous."

—ALBERT EINSTEIN

I once rented a room
in a nine-story brownstone
that buttressed the back
of a Gothic church adorned
with spiked gables and red pointed doors.
I loved how my large window
looked out at birds-eye level
at the birds and the slate roof.
I could watch stained-glass saints
loitering at all hours beneath
the vaulted apse, crowding
around the white altar
to discuss theology
or the finer points
of transubstantiation.

When it rained, the flooding roof
became medieval Paris;
when it snowed, a wedding cake
made of marzipan.
On Fridays at midnight,
the organist would release
the black and white keys
from their cage of silence
to stampede around the nave
like piebald horses.

I moved there by chance.
By chance, my father was born
in the brownstone

across the street. By chance,
(I was shaken to learn)
a nun living upstairs
was my grandfather's cousin.

No bookie would've taken odds on this.

It seemed an unknown hand
had planted me in this exact spot—
my life's dispersed loops
pulled together by a single cord
into a tidy bow,
and a weaver had exposed
his tapestry's hidden plan.

But who was going to fix
the tapestry's tangles and snares?
And what was I to do
with all the scattered signposts
pointing in one direction?

FIRESTORM

"What did you take?" they always asked
 after the broiling wall of flames,
fueled by drought and dry broom,
tore like an angry combine
through our urban woods
torching homes, cars, and trees,
even high towers of electricity—
mere toys—easy tinder
for its savage mouth.

Fear tasted like blood beating
in back of our throats.

We paused long enough
to gape at exploding bungalows
down by Lake Temescal,
each a knotty burl
bursting in the stoked-up pyre.

We took ourselves, of course—
(unlike the unlucky few
who couldn't outrun
the furious firefall).

We escaped, clutching
what we've always carried
through our dislocations—
a precious stained-glass lamp,
some books, photos, our story.

For what else do we really own
in this fragile and O
so briefly blooming world?

Except perhaps the host of a pale moon
slipping behind the veil of charcoal skies.

WEDDING POEM

(For Connie and Tom Jacobs)

When you are in love
you don't have to be perfect.
When you are in love
you can let your lover stand by you,
fully naked with your flabby belly

and weak knees, and never
be ashamed, no matter how old you are,
no matter your wrinkles or stiff joints,
no matter if the hinges of your heart
are rusty or never opened before.

Your heart quickened
when your beloved first appeared
and dared to step through
that red door, sparking
in you a frisson of hope—

Are you the one,
or must I wait
for another?

But now you both are astonished
as confetti of laughter
ripples through your house
and you know, unmistakably, even
as your teaspoon of days lessens,

that today you travel deeper
toward each other into a miracle,
despite the ticking clock,
into mornings dusted with the gold
of dailiness, into lives enfolded by love.

SEEING DANIEL BERRIGAN
FOR THE FIRST TIME

Freshly sprung from Danbury jail,
he slipped behind the altar,
wearing no clergy collar
but a black turtleneck and stole.
He was raw and modest,
a newborn chrysalis
tendering cold air.

Prison had carved trenches
into his face: well-won stripes
from waging peace. Living
the prophet's dilemma,
the two-edged sword of truth
cut his bones first before others.

When he looked at me, the pain
behind his coal-black eyes
seared my peace—miners' lamps
digging down the dark.
They mirrored Christ's cries.

Like Peter at cockcrow,
I flinched
and looked away.

DIPTYCH FOR DAVID

(For my brother, David Currie Lee: 1953–1995)

1.

Snow flurries sift down
as I trudge to a chapel
by the Charles River.

This Christmas Eve
my young brother lies dying,
his perfect body breaking—
my heart too helpless to pray.

No Christ comes
to raise my Lazarus
from the bier of his hospital bed
or my faith from my barrow of unbelief.

"Night is a thin time
and sleep
is a thin place,"
a monk in the chapel said.

The place between
the living and the dead
is more slender still—
a sliver's space away from God—
a paper cut apart from grace.
The distance between the ear
and the word, my heart and my face.

There by the altar stone,
the Creed, and the guttering light,
I taste the ashes of my own dread,
the salt-spill of tears.
Though you're not yet dead,
my heart silently keens.

2.

Gasping machines push
the billows of your lungs.
You're trapped
in your body's long box.

Beside your bed
I say your name,
watch how you struggle
and pound from the inside
to get out—your grimace
my only sign
of your frantic attempt
to surface.

Dear mountaineer,
this is the highest summit
you never reached.

Your pale lips flutter briefly
to say a word
then sink slowly, slowly
like a white flag
beneath the black tide.

THE FACTORY OF MAKING

A plump black bumblebee
zigzags through morning air
searching for the perfect flower.
He finds a wide pink rose
and scrambles through the ruffles
of her petticoat, pushes his belly
inside her secret center,
greedily taking the best she can offer
like a beggar in a Bronx deli
slipping salamis up his sleeve.

And then, though he has flown
to the center of the universe
and tasted the nectar of gods,
his work is not yet done,
for he must hasten
to the gray factory of making
where he must let go of everything
he has ever learned of cool
blue mornings, satin petals,
and even the delicate dance
of passion and watch it all change
before his eyes, helped
by an army of unseen hands
until something golden
and foreign is born
which feeds many people.

At the end, the poet asks,
Did I do that?

SOWING SEED

A muddy tractor in spring:
the driver cuts clods
of wet clay, furrowing the field,
pleating it into ribbons
of black corduroy.

A flock of hungry gulls
follows close behind, like a codicil
or a bridal veil,
plucking life
from the rutted ground.

Each day, I wake
with a gullish hunger
and leave behind a trail of white paper,
grubbing
from my own field.

I sift through piles of raw words,
sorting and stripping them clean
down to the nub
of pure meaning,
then weigh each golden kernel
in my palm

planting it in just the right place,
hoping to sow each syllable,
not as plugs smelted from dead stone,
but as good seed
pushing up
against the dense dark.

VAN GOGH'S SOWER WITH THE SETTING SUN

Late afternoon in Arles, Vincent
props his canvas in the open air
and paints a sower, his clothes
crumpled as a plowed field
as he strides along a loamy gutter
tossing his pittance of seed
under a setting sun.

The painting shows Van Gogh's soul
split in two, between his brightest joy
and a violent gloom,
plagued as he was by blind men
and demons who drove him
to eat fresh paint.

His highest passion—to feel the bliss
of color bleeding in his veins:
emerald green and marigold,
crimson and cobalt blue.

Today, his art quickens the space
around us, tosses our assumptions
out with the trash,
forcing us to see inside out

to hear colors, tints and hues
as symphony and serenade,
to taste with our eyes
the river Rhone, sharp as absinthe,

to dwell in a world without winter,
to gaze as eddies of spiraled stars
whirl their flaring tails
into song.

Even as his days darken,
Vincent paints a yellow-ochre sun
fierce as a giant sunflower,
imperious as a blazing lion;
he paints it shaking its mane.

Sun-drops explode
like golden shrapnel
over clumps of lavender clay,
over the weary planter trudging
on harrowed ground. Heaven casts
a trillion grains of light

like mustard seeds,
scattering light by lavish fistful.

THE DOUBLE OPENING

1.

Sometimes, I want to roll
and mold the words of a poem
like butterballs in my palm,
touch my tongue
to their honey-rimmed sound,
aching to eat sheer beauty.

In spring, I want to breathe
the scent of plum blossoms
deep into my lungs,
to convert the pale petals
into azure air.

Imagine how Eve must have felt
her first spring in Paradise.
Perhaps it was a pear,
not an apple, that she took—
not for pride or gluttony—

but to assuage the bright agony
she felt as she saw how lush
and lovely it looked, hanging
in singular simplicity,
a golden teardrop.

Maybe she was the first poet
to feel our awful plight—
to have a human soul
that hungers, but lacks
a double opening.

2.

Simone Weil said our soul
is like "two birds sitting in a tree—
one eats the fruit,
the other looks at it."
Neither can behold both
at the same time.

Only in heaven can we eat
what ravishes us.

I see you, poor Simone, so lonely—
a starved sparrow perched
on the tip of your tree,
hoping to reverse the work of Eve.
How urgently you sing!

You open wide your beak. You keep looking,
looking deep into the sky's pure sea,
thirsting for its blueness, singing
as if song was food enough
to fill your frail body

until finally you die, famished
for the feast of heaven.

CARRIERS OF STRANGE FIRE

"Then Aaron's sons, Nadab and Abihu, each took his fire pan and put fire in it, set incense on it, and presented strange fire before the Lord."

—LEVITICUS 10:1

Driving to Olema, past trees
sloughing their snaky skins,
over crisp leaves snapping
like crackers, I slowed
by a ribbon of fire—
a controlled burn.

Down the ravine, thick white smoke
banked above the scorched scrub
and red manzanita, shouldering
its way toward the blue coast—
a body bent
on stubborn purpose.

Between the charred-black field
and stubby flames (orange mice
nibbling the cake of macadam road),
three firemen strode. Each one
tossed fire to the ground
from a drip torch.

Fire flared behind and before
but like the three young men
who sang in Babylon's furnace,
they were not consumed.

Could I pass such a test,
singing a song
in some other flame?

An inner voice replied,
Dare to dance into the fire.

*Once inside, you will learn,
how the dark, strange fire
carries you.*

II

AND ISAIAH SAID

(For Dr. Roderick B. Dugliss)

The golden drum of a harvest moon
hangs on the rim
of my night's horizon—
soundings of new beginnings.

Questions arise—
how do I find true ground?
How do I claim my voice
after years of fear and dust,
silent as a dim pulsar
in a sea of stars?

They say the Maori
speak only from the ground
where their placenta is buried,
where one day their bones
will lie down
in that final berth.

What would it take to speak
from that ground?
To let my ripe tongue
find its talent for telling?

Isaiah, old priest in the temple,
shrank behind his scrolls and thuribles
when the call suddenly flared up.

The diamond-robed density filled
deep space, rising
bigger than Andromeda,

as the six-winged seraphs—
bright pinwheels of glory,
flew to his face

bearing the hot coal of Christ,
the Tao, the Torah,
the unuttered, unlettered Word,
and seared his lips.

Smudged clean by ashes
of adoration, two words
fell like embers from his mouth.

Words born bone-deep
echo over and over in my mind:

Send me.

SHAKER CHAIR

The chair is so clean
so straight, it looks starched,
as if carved by the hands of angels—
a chair stout enough
for God to sit on Sundays.

It stands still as history
yet gleams with the sheen
of white linen. The sturdy seat,
the erect timber of legs
could hold for centuries.

What was the cost
of crafting such a thing?
A simplicity that scoured
all chaff from the heart—
a rectitude that made the nimble hand
know how to will one thing.

ROSEBUSH IN EARLY SUMMER

An amber rosebush
poses coyly
on a whitewashed fence.
You can almost believe

God is a baker who shapes
sugared rosettes
for a wedding cake
or maybe a farmer
who grows ruffled plums.

It's as if the clumsy sun
has dribbled drops of golden syrup,
a flock of orange doves
has fluttered down,

or maybe Brahms
composed each blossom
as a song
only children hear.

If heaven exists, I do not think
it's a place of fluffy clouds
and, God forbid, mawkish hymns.
Maybe it's a glowing garden
ravished by roses more fire than flower

where angels do all the pruning,
where slugs eat only weeds,
and where Christ himself works
as head Gardener—this time
fully recognized.

ALWAYS AUTUMN

(On reading John Donne's Christmas Day sermon of 1624)

If Donne had his way,
there would be no buds
or flowers in heaven—
only fruit, plump and ripe
from the first.

"In heaven," he said,
"it is always Autumn;
God's mercies are ever
in maturity."

Heaven as bonanza,
as bumper crop,
not of harrowing or planting
but of sheaves bursting
from buff-colored knobs
brimming with blackbirds,
agitated turkeys
and bucks cropping
the tops of golden stubble.

A land of crabapples
and cranberries,
pumpkins and persimmons,
of quail coveys
crying by coils of hay
and starlings swirling
above the withered stooks.

A Promised Land
where hot-baked bread
becomes manna—
and cider decants
from Cana.

A land where boughs
of yellow ginkgo
bend with gold coins
held in their hands,
ready to scatter freely
to all in want.

A PRIESTLY PRAYER

(After John Donne)

Pound and knead me, O God,
with the palm of your powerful hand.
Stir up the batter of my soul;
better me with the salt of your Spirit,
the yeastbite of new birth,
then lift me up and kindle me
in the white-hot oven
of your love
till I rise into living bread,
consumed by the passion of your Christ,
broken, shredded, and scattered
to feed your famished people.

THE GOLDEN STRING

I give you the end of a golden string.
Only wind it into a ball,
It will lead you to Heaven's gate
Built into Jerusalem's wall.

—WILLIAM BLAKE, JERUSALEM,
THE EMANATION OF THE GIANT ALBION

It takes some a lifetime
to find the golden string,
to hold the slender thread of light
in their hand, gentle
as a prayer, feeling the pulse
of life pulling them forward.

Some people, of course, have never heard
of the golden string, or if heard,
have not believed it
and shut their ears
to the nonsense of the unknown.
Some have longed and hoped for it
but have so closed their rebel hearts
they can never find it.

No one can give you the golden string.
You must search it out yourself.
You must learn to let go, to free fall
into that circle of solitude
called waiting.
Even your mastery and your prayer
will burden you.

Ambition
snaps the thread.

When you die, if you want
you can catch the end
of the golden string
when it passes by, over and over

and you will discover
it's the golden river
you've been walking on
all along.

THE WATCHERS

Where do we go when we die?
What happens after the rush of smooth air
stops
between our frozen teeth?

Some rare souls glimpse
Paradise before they go.
Blake, for instance, entertained
the Archangel Gabriel
one summer night in his study.

That star-dazzled being
opened the roof of his house
and whisked him to the sun,
then nudged the round world
with one finger
and made it move.

If it was me, maybe I'd ask
an impulsive question:
*Please sir, tell me
what do you do
all day in heaven?*

And he'd say, making the air
jiggle with mirth,

*Why, don't you know?
We watch you.*

FOR SOME DEATH COMES

For some death comes
like a skinny old lady
frantically winding her clock
and bleating the time of day,
but not for me.

For some death comes
like a low-flying jockey
riding high on a drugged horse
with all the races won,
but not for me.

For some death comes
like a sun that rises in the West
then blows out like a bulb
leaving naked stars dangling in the dark,
but not for me.

Death comes heavily for some,
but for me, he sings of life
like an Irish tenor
and softly opens the door
to my bridal chamber.

WHAT IF THE WORLD WAS WIDER

"The World is not this little cottage of Heaven and Earth."
—Thomas Traherne, Centuries of Meditations

What if the world, dear as it is,
was wider than this cottage
of heaven and earth?
Wider than our penny's worth of patchwork sky,
our tiny marble of blue marl?

It's hard to imagine anything more—
so accustomed are we to this hutch,
even though, each year, the cellar floods
and bilge water paints graffiti on the basement walls.
Car fumes smudge the windows with flecks of black snuff,
rats infest the thatch, wind rips the roof,
and the foundations crack like a half-baked crumb cake.

But who could want anything more,
what with lanes of linden and lilac,
the wild horses racing unafraid,
the ebullient speech of brooks pursuing their own message,
clusters of hazy stars, lofting birds, glowering mountains,
wedges of blue glaciers crunching stones like glass,
the rash extravagance of rainbows or honeybees,
and the flaring canopies of Aurora Borealis?

But what if the world was wider
than our green terrarium,
this giant snow globe,
our breathing emerald
shielded in God's hand?

What if death was friend, not foe,
more midwife than executioner,
pushing us to plunge deeper
into the river of light, into a life reborn
but unknown?

What would we find there? Life the same
but on a higher plane? Honest lawyers?
Generous bankers? Thin bakers?
Toothless lions eating tofu?
Sharks turned into laughing dolphins?
Would Yeshiva and Sunday School
still meet? What about the PTA?
I expect everyone would join the union.

Because the union would be all there is—
gathering all things into one,
the way the solar winds roll
sparks of being into coils of fire.
In that wider world, roses will sing,
calling us to dance
out of our mortal skins
and exchange them for gowns of light.

DUINO REVISITED

Do you remember the story of Soyuz 7?
How after 155 days of whirling in space,
six cosmonauts were blinded
by a bright orange light
carrying seven flying figures,

(their titanic wings long as jetliners)
glowing like seven filaments—
each a bright bulb of being.

Twice, this squad of angels
with gilded wings,
eyes lit with blue flame,
followed the spaceship for ten minutes
in hushed flight, each smiling like Buddha—
then disappeared.

Who knows what the spacemen saw
as they flew like wingless birds
in the bottled air of their capsule?

Did they really see angels?
Or was it just the reflected glory
of their interior sight?

Chances are,
when they landed,
each one touched the ground

most tenderly.

THE KERASTION

(In memory of Dr. Roussel Sargent)

A long leather flute
made from skin
flayed from a human body.
No tune is heard
from this shaft of suffering;
its hidden music
is the stilled heart
remembering.

But if you do hear,
you know your ears
have opened
like seashells

to rose petals drifting down,
snails twisting
out of their china caravans,
seahorses neighing
beneath the rolling waves,
and even the sound
of green moss weeping
in the evening.

There is only one way
you can hear the Kerastion,
but sadly, no one else will know—
when the ashes
of your abandoned body
melt into the simple sea.

WHY THANKSGIVING DAY WILL NEVER BE THE SAME

(After Billy Collins)

In a wide meadow
a flock of wild turkeys
totters knock-kneed in single file,
a band of Puritans
in long black coats with tails.

They lurch forward with hunched shoulders
and long, scrawny necks—
a parade of Ichabod Cranes
en route to a dinner of gruel, lentils,
and sour milk. Or better yet,
to hear the whole Book of Leviticus
read aloud at once,

or to the chopping block.

Maybe it's predestination.

Of course, they know deep in their DNA
that they or their progeny
will end up sooner or later
on a Thanksgiving platter
unless the president
grants them a pardon—
as he's pardoned
several turkeys already.

I wonder if Jesus had them in mind
when he spoke the first beatitude:
"Blessed are the poor in spirit,
for theirs is the kingdom of heaven."

You can't get any poorer
than a dead turkey, all stuffed
and trussed,

even if you put cranberries in it.

THE PROMISED LAND

"Pay attention, Israel, and be careful to do this so that it may go well with you and that you may increase greatly in number—as the Lord, God of your ancestors, said to you, you will have a land flowing with milk and honey."

—DEUTERONOMY 6:3

Kierkegaard said, "To dare
is to lose one's footing
momentarily. Not to dare
is to lose oneself."

So you lean into deeper dark—
your heart, a turbine
of hope and terror.

The only thing you cling to
is the promise—
a silver thread
in your trembling hands,
a rescue line,
a happy ending.

It carries you like a rosary
through your first step
across the abyss.
But then,
you have to let go

of the promise.

MAGNOLIA BLUES

Twelve angry jays perch
all at once in our magnolia tree.
Two gangs of bullies dressed in blue
chase each other limb to limb,
squawking and cursing
like washerwomen
across the clotheslines.

They charge and dive
in their clattery territorial dance,
bursting like sapphire sparks
from the green tongues of leaves
as flowers and hand grenades
of dry seed pods
drop harmlessly to earth below.

I don't know
why wars have to happen.
Of course, our wars are crueler
than blue jays squabbling
over precious space in a tree.

When we fly, we drop pods
of death that do not fall gently
in the night. We never see
the fruit of our destruction,
but swoop down on metal wings
like flame-throwing dragons,
then soar away leaving nothing
but burnt husks of what cities
used to be.

PRAYER OF THE HERMIT CRAB

O God, undo me.
Break me from my grudging bonds,
like bones grown and bent
in splints poorly done, to a straighter freedom
where the torch of sunlight
expands my soul
so that I, skittish as a hermit crab
scuttling to a new shell,
never shrink
from any move of nature—

especially Your own.

III

THE FOUNTAIN AND THE TOWER

1. The Chalice Well[2]

Overlapping circles cover
the well, its sides lavish
with baby tears, spongy moss,
and hanging fern fronds.

They call this place,
this blood spring, holy.
Over the red rock
sacred waters have flowed

for two thousand years.
Rusty water brims up
and slides down to entwining pools
centered in a plush garden.

Meanwhile, the yew trees climb
the hollow hill like black friars
from another race, telling their beads,
whispering spells from Arthur's past.

Come now, go with haste.
Come shelter under the shadow
of this red rock. Come drink
at the lion's place.

There at last, between the lion
and the rose,
I drink and find real grace.

2. Tower Bells of Glastonbury

One autumn day, crabbed
and queer as Avalon's fame,
bell ringers from Hampshire
came to the church tower
of John the Baptist.

For two hours, the wind-weathered walls
of Glastonbury town ricocheted
with sound. The ringers tugged
and pulled their cotton sallied teats,
milking Grandsire Triples
till the leaden peals
dropped like pearls
to the stony streets.

No one in town much cared.
They strolled, they carped
and quibbled
over the butcher's cut of meat.
Some merchants dared complain
about the tower's tolling.

But I, a spirit-starved pilgrim,
a grayling after God,
came longing for quicksilver
to waken my soul.

At the chapel's core,
where Gothic arches
brace heaven's blue roof
by a mute altar and a chiseled Christ
(his arms outstretched, utterly giving),
I felt a stone roll away
from the cave of my heart.

Suddenly bells cascaded
in a cataract of sound, tolling
round and round, welling my heart
with joy and the ringing.

Then from behind,
a far-off sound singing.

DISTILLING THE CORE

What is prayer
but the hollow scrape
of a spoon
on the bottom
of a wooden bowl?

What is prayer
but the sound
of secret music
opening deaf ears
of a muzzled soul?

What is prayer
but the climbing into bed
between silken sheets
of silence
and resting there.

What is prayer
but the gathering
of a thousand energies
into one tiny
pin-prick
of
praise.

PALM SUNDAY 1212

1.

That year came like Apostles,
in twelves.

2.

One moonlit midnight
like a deer stepping
from a dusky forest,
St. Clare came.

3.

All my fresh springs
are in you. St. Clare—
the spark
in everyone's eyes.

4.

When the blonde hair
fell on the floor
like straw,
wings and songs
were heard in the bells
of St. Mary of the Angels.

5.

Sister Lark,
who wears a cowl
like a religious,
looked up and sang
from the brown earth.

6.

Outside, all the guardians
of Umbria—those poor angels
(skinny and small,
or fat with garlic
in their mustaches)
danced and prayed
for a good harvest
for the people.

THE KEEPER OF JULIAN'S SHRINE

(In memory of the Rev. Robert Llewelyn: 1909-1998)

Like a long black lance he stood—
all cassock, clawed
by prayer and poverty,
a creaking tower of praise,
of humility and good.

Nuns in blue bowed down
like toadstools
as his rattle-boned fingers
raised the round Host high,
arms aching
to hoist the world up to heaven,
where he himself was halfway hidden.

Later, we met to talk
of hallowed things,
of Julian and God,
there in his close-cluttered cell
joined by a chorus of icons
interceding for us
from his whitewashed walls.

When this priest spoke of Christ
his coal-spot eyes blazed,
his tongue became a tong of fire.

Suddenly the sun tore away
the gray, bloated clouds
and shone through the window,
highlighting his elfish ears—
his antennae of the human heart.

Fear made me shiver
as I saw his soul:
the last of the Old Ones
from the Hollow Hills.

GLEANING FOR GOOSEBERRIES

March scowls like an old English lady
with a winter larder low on jams.

The farmer down West Lambrook Lane
lets his grove gutters drain,
then invites his neighbors
and even us to bring
our baskets to glean
what his pickers haven't seen.

So we young sisters come
in woolen habits to pick
the fruits of our uncertain spring.
If you saw us in town,
our wicker baskets made us seem
like maids from an older Christendom.

Only our Wellington boots
resound against the cobbled street
as ice cracking against stone water.

Inside the gooseberry grove
the hired hand shouts and waves his cap.
Sisters, you can pick the rows down yonder;
There be more in them bushes.
With pickers, Fridays have a way of leaving
more on the bush than in the hand.

This Somerset March fills our laps
with emeralds. Like the rich,
we jam our reserves—

the joy of another man's Yes.

COMPLINE

Compline is Mary's time.
The night breathes deep,
forever blue.

Brimming candles
open eyes of honey
in the dark.

We five nuns in brown
bow down, round as stones
before God's face.

Daily, we see drunks in gutters,
feed hungry children, tear-streaked
and hardened by fear.

Lord, you are in the midst of us
and we are called by Your name.
Do not forsake us,
O Lord our God

Compline. The lily near Our Lady
arches its languid neck
like a love song.

Starlight on a moonless night
shows where Mary's feet
have stepped among us.

Where her instep was laid,
only scent of lilies remains.

A TROUBADOUR ROMANCE

You were once the future
foretold to me by a psychic
from a colony of clairvoyants
pitched by the foggy banks
of the St. John's River,
a swamp-water outpost
between this world and the next.

A place where long gray beards
of Spanish moss
catch spirits in midair.

I remember her kitchen table,
the red-checkered tablecloth,
how she closed her eyes
and gazed into dark space
scrying beneath the scrim of time.

"The lover you will meet," she said,
"will be at the North Sea."

And so it was—four years later.
How many turns it took
to overtake my fate!

As Franciscans, we met secretly
by holy Lindisfarne
on a Northumbrian beach.
Later, you wooed me with poems
and the sounds of Elgar.
I'd go to bed aching for you
but cried the name of Jesus
in my sleep.

In Greyfriars Chapel, straddling
the River Stour, I stole glances
with you during Compline.
I loved the tilt of your head
as you listened, how you'd stride
among those ancient stones
in your brown robe and cincture,
a modern bearded troubadour,
your lustrous eyes pulling people to you,
irresistible as the lunar tide.

When it was time for me to fly home,
you ran by the window of our van
as long as you could,
waving a dramatic goodbye.
I sat inside silent, tearful,
looking away.

More than forty years gone,
I live a love-filled life
in another country,
but every decade or so
I try to see your face
(fading like a Kodak photo)
and hear the distant strains
of Elgar's *Nimrod*—violins
swell and recede, waves of longing
lap against the weird enigma
of time and space.

TO OUR LADY OF THE REDWOODS

(After Thomas Merton)

O sisters of Whitethorn,
you sisters of a white martyrdom,
come eternally from Our Lady's forests.

Open your doors to uncharted paths
and bow like windy grass
before God's name. Everything
you touch is renewed.

Sisters of Whitethorn,
you die and do not die,
drinking the wine of a thousand silences,
tasting the bread of kindred solitude.

We know God is holy
because the air around your house
smells like honey.

God has given you many scrolls to eat.
Do not disappoint his prophets.

When you sing, the redwoods listen with joy.
When you pray, the gray wolf lies down
and eats camellias at your door.

ELEGY FOR A MONK

(In memory of Fr. Roger De Ganck OCSO)

His guttural Belgian tongue
mangled English
like he was gargling marbles.

A scholar, poet, and secret mystic,
he once showed me his poems—
but alas, they were in Flemish.
He'd walk bird-like to chapel,
stooping over his cane, wearing
a black beret, his pipe and pouch
of tobacco bulging in his denim smock.

Late afternoons, Beethoven
was good company for him
and the visiting fox.
His milky eyes missed
the wild iris by the brook
but he knew every birdsong
high in the redwoods.
Once, he fell, then had to say Mass
one-handed, wearing a sling
for his broken wing.

Once, I impetuously kissed
his spotty gray cheek
at the passing of the peace.
Days later, at home writing poems,

his kiss returned (I don't know how),
falling lightly from the poised air,
brushing my cheek from afar—

falling
like a benediction,

falling
like a farewell.

AN UNEXPECTED VISIT

(In memory of Sr. Godilieve Theys OCSO)

The old nun hears knocking
and says, "Come in,"
but no one comes. Again,
she hears a knock—
but no one is there.
Maybe it's a woodpecker
drilling a hole in the roof,
an impish ghost pulling a prank?

Maybe it's death (polite for once)
knocking first so not to startle.
A secret instinct makes her turn
toward the glass door.
A tawny doe stands before her
soft-eyed, erect as a salute,
rapping the wooden deck
with her hoof.

What if the deer nudges
the door open and steps inside
to eat lambent lilies on the desk?

What if she kneels down
and lays her long graceful neck,
those fur-tufted ears, in her lap?
(No doubt, at ninety-two the nun
is still a virgin—but you never know.)

What if she rests there
for the longest time, sighs,
then climbs onto her stilts
and walks out the door,
flicking her tail as a sign?

JACOB AT PENIEL

*"Come, O Thou Traveler unknown,
whom still I hold but cannot see."*

—Charles Wesley

Barefaced, wild-winged,
he dove from heaven's ropes
landing on me as if I was water:
Death's dark angel come for me!

I rolled and fought against his grip.
I slid beneath his wings,
clasped my arms around his waist
feeling the soft thud of feathers,
wingbones beating my back,
felt the rip of his muscles, smelled
his hot sweat upon my face.

When he threw me to the ground,
I grabbed his thigh; when he twisted
my arm, I struck his knee—each time
the awful shadow slipped away.

All night, we grappled shoulder
to shoulder, panting face to face,
our bodies entwined
more lovers than fighters.

Both of us refused to fail—
until he lay his head
upon the ground, his eyes
fixed past the burning stars.

Let me go, for it is break of day.
Then he touched my hip,
like potter to clay,
and wrenched it askew.

But I would not let him go unblessed,
wringing from defeat some shred of grace.
I lost but won a new name, a chance
to glimpse God's face. At dawn he left
pressing down the air with dusty wings.
I limped back to our tents, naming the place.

Fire-forged, I rise from the blows.

THE TENT OF MEETING

No one expected anything strange that day
as they watched Moses push aside
the folds of white and blue indigo
to step from the tent of meeting
onto the hot desert sand and walk
through a pillar of cloud.

Suddenly, his face gushed light—
another burning bush—so strong
people had to shield their eyes
from Adonai's dazzle.

This is what happens
when two souls (or many)
catch fire—

as when you, dear friend, rise
to meet me with gentle courtesy.
A matching light flickers in your face.

And doesn't recognition
always startle us—
like a bee sting
or a spark from heaven?

WHEN ROSES BORE BERRIES

"When the steward tasted the water that had become wine..."
—JOHN 2:1-12

I used to hate weddings—until Cana,
what with the incessant drone
of drums, timbrels, and shawms
and the god-awful clash of two families
and a town under one tent for a week.
It's a wonder they could eat for the stench!
The bride was much too young,
doe-eyed and nauseous from nerves,
with chains of gold like shackles around her neck.
(Imagine being palmed off by greedy parents like that!)

Then there was the groom, long
past first manhood, looking pale
and evasive, sweaty with lust,
and his mother, reeking
of garlic, eyeing her in-laws charily,
while the sotted father—
his fingers slick with grease—
fiddled with the female dancers,
always shouting his toasts
and waving his cup for more.

I pitied the bleary-eyed servers
racing like harried dogs
to and from the kitchen, stealing
scraps of meat whenever they could,
fetching platters filled with joints
of roasted lamb garnished with rosemary
and carrying jugs of plonk.

O sure, I'd tasted lots of good wine before
as steward to wealthy priests and merchants
(and even a tax collector or two).

But at Cana, Jesus' wine was different.
When his wine first touched my lips
I tasted stars.

Even now, I can taste the red ruby drops,
melted pomegranates in my mouth.
This wine was so perfect, so pure,
it was like drinking bottled song.

Dense with opulent flavors—
blackest cherry, currants and cassis
mixed with roses and hints of plum
tinted with tobacco and tar,
aged in casks of oak, hewn
from the oldest oak on earth,
this wine led me beyond myself
to the edge of heaven—a wine
vinted not simply to sip,
but meant to be pilgrimage.

Later, when they told me
how he'd touched the jars
and changed the water into wine,
I felt real fear. Who was I
to be chosen as taster?
Me, with my life, stale
as flat beer, with all the joy
bled out of it as if by leeches?

No, I never tasted such wine,
nor feared again—until the full moon
that final Pesach, where, at table,

graciously and sadly,
he gave us another wine-filled cup—
this time turned to blood.

A POEM FOR THE FEAST
OF CHRIST THE KING

See how this infant boy
lifted himself down
into his humble crèche
and laid his tender glove of skin
against splintered wood—
found refuge in a rack
of straw—home
that chilly dawn, in sweetest
silage, those shriven stalks.

This outcast king lifted
himself high upon his savage cross,
extended the regal banner
of his bones, draping himself
upon his throne—his battered feet,
his wounded hands not fastened
there by nails but sewn
by the strictest thorn of love.

ADVENT

(On a theme by Dietrich Bonhoeffer)

Look how long
the tired world waited,
locked in its lonely cell,
guilty as a prisoner.

As you can imagine,
it sang and whistled in the dark.
It hoped. It paced and puttered about,
tidying its little piles of inconsequence.

It wept from the weight of ennui
draped like shackles on its wrists.
It raged and wailed against the walls
of its own plight.

But there was nothing
the world could do
to find its freedom.
The door was shut tight.

It could only be opened
from the outside.

Who could believe the latch
would be turned by the flower
of a newborn hand?

ZECHARIAH'S ANNUNCIATION

"Zechariah said to the angel, 'How can I be sure of this?'"
—Luke 1:18

It was not to Elizabeth (you realize)
that the angel came,
treading down the stair of muslin air
thick with resin incense,
but to Zechariah, her husband—
the rural priest and pragmatist
doing his yearly turn of duty
by the altar in Herod's Temple.

His body froze, as Gabriel
knew it would, when the syllables
of grace poured like liquid fire
from his lips: "Fear not!"
(Angels always carry warning signs
for these events.)
What he didn't expect
was a heart clenched like a fist
against good news.

Zechariah's doubt turned his tongue
to stone—was forced to gestate
in its womb of silence
nine months long, waiting
like the Rock of Meribah
to be smitten, cracked open
by birth and the strict staff
of the living Word.

Only Gabriel knew how that tongue,
once purified, would birth
pure praise, poetry unstuttered—
ringing prophecy—

giving to his son, at last,
the true name
he never found
for himself.

THE LANGUAGE OF ANGELS

"If I speak in the tongues of men and angels..."
—1 Corinthians 13:1

How did the angels speak
the night God unzipped
heaven's sky dome to reveal
a floor show of the angelic chorus
on a floodlit stage in paradise
with its backdrop of blue sky,
lush green fields, stone walls,
trees, hedges, and brooks
like the rolling hills
of Dorset or Devon.

To the shepherds of Palestine
they spoke in old Aramaic.
To us, they speak like King James
or the Revised Standard Version,
though some get sloppy and slip
into common paraphrase.

Are they polyglots like on Pentecost?
Privately, do they speak
in glossolalia? And how
do they speak to God?
Only when spoken to?
Maybe they use no words at all
but simply beam thoughts of light?

And what about the sheep
and the black and white dog?
Didn't they see and hear
the same celestial sight?

Do angels have linguists
who specialize in barnyard
and canine, not to mention
the whole animal kingdom?

Of course, the flock all voted
to send a representative.
This is why one shepherd came
with a newborn lamb
tucked inside the folds

of his woolen cloak,
asleep like Jesus,
with a drop of milk
on its chin.

SOUNDINGS

Riviera tourists with cases of caviar
lounge on over-bloated beaches
by great gray waves of a dying sea.
From Barcelona to Sicily,
Naples to Marseilles,
they force the fish of Lyons
to flee to the deep.
Fishermen move to the hills.
Stinking nets lie barren on bitter wharves.

O little fish, little fish, where have you been?
I've been to Monaco to see the great king.
O little fish, little fish, how do you do?
My sea's like a graveyard, my shore like a slough.

Fishmonger wives make novenas.
St. Anthony sits all ears
(not to mention the holy twelve!).
Most dear and glorious saints
to whom it may concern:
Our fish are gone.
Our coasts are empty.
Our men must haul in the ocean.
They are away too long.
The Mediterranean is dead.
There is little to eat.
We cannot keep a good Lent.
Nothing but onions and bread,
garlic and bread.

We will not flaunt
our streamlined bodies in lurid attire,
our gold-plate china, our champagne meals.

We will not stare with devouring eyes
at honey-toned legs of one-night stands.
We loathe the grasping men
who rape the sea
and turn our souls to stone.

Plead for us, O Lady
of a thousand sorrows.
Weep bowls of tears
to purify our sea.

(P.S. Our Sister Water is no longer chaste.)

We thank you, Father,
for the gift of water;
for the greater waters and the small,
for the mighty waters of the sea,
for the surging waters of the sound.
We thank you for the crystal waters
that flow in bays,
the drops of emerald
that spray the shoals,
the lucid water that rests in shallows.
We thank you for the lees and eddies
that sing translucent waves
of limpid blue; we thank you
for the lunar tides and the solar swells,
for the tempest and the fathoms
of the deep. Let us bless the Lord.

Let the waters above the heavens
celebrate the Lord.
Each shower of rain and fall of dew
celebrate the Lord.
O springs of praise and forever water seas
and streams, bless the Lord.

O whales and all that move
in the waters, all that dart, burrow,
and glide in the sea, praise the Lord.

Big fish, tiny fish, jellyfish, and carp,
shiny green crabs and freshwater trout,
sunfish, starfish and barracuda shark,
redfish, cuttlefish, and moray eels,
you carnivals of mackerels
and laughing dolphins,
all scallops and oysters,
cockles and mussels
alive, alive, O
give praise to the Lord.
You barnacles and ark shells,
you Portuguese man o' war—
you blue-bottled bubbles
above pink coral gardens,
exalt him now,
and forever keep your peace.

IV

SONGS OF THE LOGOS

1. The Turning Word

It takes the third ear to hear
the Turning Word—
God's silent sacrament.

Fruit of an invisible womb,
the Turning Word rises
like a living lotus,
a persistent song
from the muddy floor
of a receiving mind—
from a stillness so deep
you can hear the stars shine.

The Turning Word
pries open all ears
like the stabbing cry of a muezzin
calling from his tower
atop the Temple Mount.

It turns and peels
the heart's skin
like a grape.

To hear the Turning Word,
all we need to undo our deafness
is assault our ears
with silence,

seek the conversion
of speech,
catch the music
of the spinning gyre.

2. God's Annunciation

They thought God would refuse.
He always had before.
To the Jews he was silent
as a glass of cold water,
that is, until he bent
to hear his own daughter.
Like Merlin and Vivian, so shrewd,
one could not tell the difference
between the wooer and the wooed.
She, the young plant, broke his indifference.
He never saw his hand in her making.
She was so perfect, so herself, so still,
that she made his heart thrill
for his own out-breaking.
Then God said yes—suffused
by love's deep aching.
(Did God get confused
as we, at his first lovemaking?)
But in the end, nothing was able
to come between us and him.
God became impregnable,
and Mary soared like the seraphim.

3. The Midnight Day Star

That night was not benevolent
when God came kneeling down—
not as sheep and oxen kneel
in their straw-packed pens,
but contented as a child
waiting to be blessed.

That windy moonless path
led the Magi on their camels
down an icy track, thwarted
by sleet, thorns, rocks,
and too many false trails
to a tavern in Bethlehem
that served sour wine
and most unsatisfactory food.

No doubt, the Magi were thrilled
when they saw the Star floating
above the cave that windborn night.
They hurried to the site and found
Mary's boy lying in a lullaby,
asleep and humble as a stranger.

Jesus never saw the star-beams
that night, dancing in the icy air.
But like the others
who came to understand,
the kings bent down
and kneeled.

4. Gauguin's Mary

La Orana Maria—soft as papaya,
light coffee brown, eyes
like the night, stands wrapped
in a blood-red pareo. Her well-weaned son
sits astride her shoulder; she holds
his foot to her breast like a locket.
Heavy with sleep, he nuzzles her hair.

Each day, she brings her unlettered boy,
Word become flesh, to a brook
to drink its sweetness. Until she comes,
the tropical Jordan waits
to stop dead in its tracks
like the Red Sea.

Bananas, mangos, melons
lie sumptuous at her feet.
Native girls stand on the water
like Christ, testing the stream
with their toes. Rainbows soar
as scarlet birds screech of dangers to come.
In the tangy jungle, the bare-bottomed
orangutans with golden eyes watch,
screened by a twisted ocean of trees.

After the monsoons,
God strolls atop volcanos,
gazing fondly on mother
and child below. Pungent gardenias
thicken the air with nutmeg and vanilla—
the alluring smell of paradise.

Entwining halos point
to an angel, yellow and blue-winged,
barefoot behind lacy blossoms
of a breadfruit tree. She waits
for Mary's fruit to ripen.

5. The Baptism

How much did he know about his God
before he plumbed the bottom
of that brown river, the frontier
of infinity, and, in a way, died there—
drowning the delusions of his youth:
the deceit of power and the mirage
of immortal blood. Did he know
that God would break the rod
against his own son?
Did he think he could woo
Ruach's fire down from heaven's lair
and tame her there as a trapper lures
a wood dove down
from a whitethorn tree?

When it's all said and done,
did he know the way of love,
even then, would mean his oblivion,
but the way of death—immortality?

No, the vision came
when the fire seized him
and the voice of God
spoke his name:
*This is my son, in whom
I am well pleased.*

After this, vinegar,
the three nails.

6. Christ in the Wilderness

Desert tossed, outcast,
flung up, high flown
to the rim of ruined souls,
he stood alone.
A callous wind blew
through his soul's core
while the primeval voice
(he knew so well)
disturbed his fast
and mocked him, saying:
*If you are the son of God,
command these stones . . .*

And he, pivoting between terror
and bliss, filled forty bowls of anguish
in reply: *How many deaths
must I die before "Who am I"
becomes "son of God"?*
Then the wind sighed
and tore apart
his heart's last hope:

*Just as these stones will shout,
so must your life
change into living bread.*

7. God, What a Wind

> *"They woke him up and said to him,*
> *'Teacher, don't you care that we are about to die?'"*
>
> —Mark 4:38

God, what a wind it was!
Wind whipped the water white.
Spray shredded the flapping sail
then cracked the yardarm in two
as the seashore fell from sight.

Fear seized our fragile boat.
Whitecaps tossed our keel into chaos
(cruel heartbeat of the whirlwind).
We clung to him: our only way across.

But wouldn't you know?
He napped through the brawl
in the stern, head
on a pillow utterly spent.

I suddenly saw and took note
of a fiercer harm that flailed our sea,
and trembled to see Mary's son
asleep in our heaving boat.

(No man could have stayed so remote.)

Terrified, I glimpsed his destiny:
his task—oceans of worlds to save.
To him, this was just another dry run
for his three days' fight
in a howling grave.

8. The Teachable Moment

> *"As she stood behind him at his feet, weeping, she began to wet his feet with her tears. She wiped them with her hair, kissed them, and anointed them with the perfumed oil."*
>
> —LUKE 7:38

It was the way she spontaneously
broke open the flask of her being,
weeping and kissing his feet,
that amazed him so.

All sense of self slipped off her
like a tattered robe, so little
did she care about her red-rimmed eyes,
her swollen face and dripping hair,
as the torrent of gratitude
burst from her used-up body.

Jesus' face
was the only one
she saw.

Simon objected, of course, for obvious reasons:
at the brazen way she'd entered his house
carrying an alabaster jar,
at the silver coins draped around her neck
flaunting her profession,
and how she touched those feet.

But Jesus, who could peel
a person like a peach
tasting the raw pulp of longing,
tendered her tears like seeds
in his own heart.

Being who he was,
he was not afraid
to be taught by a woman.

Where else did he learn
how to wash
his disciples' feet?

9. The Transfiguration

The downpour, sky-ditched,
couldn't drench the fire
that fell and clung to him
like a falcon—
tearing the air with each talon,
gashing a window to heaven.
Glory bent, he burst before our eyes
into the burning bush—
yet God in him, flesh-fed
and passion-fueled, never quenched
his manhood. His mentor, Moses,
came first, then Elijah, with a rush,
as the three sprang up
into that blaze.

Petrified, Peter cried,
Let us make three tents
to set aside this place!
(As if he could contain
the grace of God like that!)

Then the cloud, darker
than death, descended
and from it, God's echo rebounded:
This is my beloved son,
listen to him,
my son. My son.

Then he stood alone.

10. The Passion Tree

Ripe blood drops like fruit
from the tree. No sweeter fruit
could there be in a grove
where the Gardener bathes
the soil of new birth
with his blood. Crops
don't take much water
from the earth as he gives
in his own spilling. Such
was the risk of love,
to become bad fruit
for our pardoning.
Then the fruit that fell like berries
was gathered up by three Marys.

They trudge home
under a shroud of clouds.

11. Resurrection

Think how much it cost him
to have his shoreless slumber shattered—
to sleep, quiet as a hymn,
then wake, startled
by that clattering blast.
What fear must have pierced him,
so soon swung down from the cross,
as the mighty air grasped him
back to life. This life, new birth for us,
but a second death for him,
of sorts. What happened? Did he combust,
as fire bursts from waiting wood, as cherubim
break into brighter being before God,
blending their wings in one exultant hymn?
Or did he bend his body down
so far, his dust became another Adam?

He comes tranquil as dawn,
walking through the tender grass
on wounded feet—secret as a trespasser,
humble as a pilgrim, voyager
from the Promised Land.

Even in this, he assumes nothing.
Such it is to be God.

12. The Stone of Grief

"Mary stood weeping outside the tomb..."
JOHN 20:15-16

For days, the stone of grief
hung from a noose around my neck
heavy, gray and hard
as a millstone,
with its hollowed core
mirroring my own.

Its weight plunged me
into fathoms of tears.
A whale of darkness
swallowed me,
the stone's weight
crushed my breath.

Sleepless and numb, I climbed
down the rocky path that dawn
to his newly hewn tomb
with my basket of aloes and myrrh.
Gone! The soldiers were gone
and that huge stone
strangely shoved away.

It tore my heart's curtain
in two.

I fled in fear to find Peter and John.
We raced as one pulse
to that awful place.

Nothing there but blood-stained strips
dropped on cold, smooth stone,
and the sweat-cloth,
once wrapped around his face,
folded like swaddling clothes.

I stayed behind, hugging
my stone of grief—
the only part of him
I could still hold.

Woman, why are you weeping?

They've taken away my Lord,
I don't know where
they have laid him.
Tell me, so I can bathe him
with aloes and myrrh,
touch his hands,
see his face one last time—
already I'm forgetting
what he looks like.

Then, *Mary!*
And I turned to the light.

13. Emmaus

"He said to them, 'What things?'"

—Luke 24:19³

As if he didn't know
he'd been a pawn
in Pilate's Passover play,
know full well each driven nail

that pierced his wrists and feet,
that bound his body to iniquity.
And yes, even know that sharp
inrush of light that preceded
his first sip of sacred air.

Yet he strolled down
that thirsty road,
an anonymous teacher.
He'd opened Scripture to us,
peeling back the Torah
layer by layer,

inscribing our hearts
with a stylus of fire,
each word pointing to himself.

Can you guess who I am now?

That night, we pressed him
to stay and eat at a crowded inn
where merchants haggled
over shekels by the fire.

At table, what did we see?
Wounds previously hidden?
Or was it the way
the bread was broken?

Instantly, he opened the eyes
of our grieving hearts,
lifting the lid of surprise,
revealing himself
undisguised.

Then he vanished,
as salt seasons flour,
into wheat.

14. The Ascension

Not to go up,
but into everything he went—
just as leaven is spent
in the dough's rising.
Why, he even made the halls
of hell repent.
So, it's not surprising
he made our hearts ascend
like wells springing up
from desert sand, like song
bursting from a starling.
With Christ's vanishing
all creation was reborn.

Joy alone shows his place of hiding.

NOTES

1. Whitfield Peter. *Sir Francis Drake (Historic Lives)*. New York: New York University Press, 2004, 77.

2. The cover of the Chalice Well in Glastonbury, England, was designed by the church architect and archaeologist, Frederick Bligh Bond. He used an ancient sacred geometric symbol called the *Vesica Piscis*, which means "bladder of a fish." The central almond shape is a mandorla, which represents the seed of life. The overlapping circles are a yonic symbol of the feminine. See Mann, Nicholas, and Fletcher, Paul. "The Story of the Cover for the Chalice Well." *The Chalice* (Spring 2007) 9-12.

3. According to the Gospel of John, Cleopas and his wife Mary were the uncle and aunt of Jesus of Nazareth. His aunt was present at Jesus' crucifixion. See John 19:25: "Meanwhile, standing near the cross of Jesus were his mother, and his mother's sister, Mary the wife of Clopas, and Mary Magdalene." Cleopas, with an alternate spelling, and another unknown person—possibly his wife Mary—are mentioned in Luke's story of walking on the road to Emmaus. See Luke 24:13-35.

PAMELA CRANSTON WAS BORN in New York City and raised in Deerfield, Massachusetts. She studied Russian history and journalism at Stetson University from 1968 to 1971, where she was editor of *The Reporter*, the school's weekly newspaper.

In 1974, she traveled to Somerset, England, to become the first American to join the Community of St. Francis (CSF)—Franciscan first order nuns in the Anglican Communion associated with the Society of St. Francis (SSF). Later, she transferred to the first American CSF house in San Francisco. While there in community, she worked on skid row, did jail ministry, served the homeless through the Catholic Worker, and helped Latina refugees. After leaving the order in 1978, she helped start the Episcopal Sanctuary for the homeless in San Francisco and worked in the alcoholism recovery field as a counselor and administrator for the San Francisco Public Health Department.

In 1984, she received a bachelor of arts degree from San Francisco State University in inter-disciplinary social science, gerontology, and creative writing. In 1988 she received a master of divinity degree, with distinction, from the Church Divinity School of the Pacific (CDSP) in Berkeley, California. Ordained as an Episcopal priest in 1990, she has served several San Francisco Bay area churches and hospices for the past thirty years.

Her books include a novel, *The Madonna Murders* (St. Huberts, 2003), and *Coming to Treeline: Adirondack Poems* (St. Huberts, 2005) Her poems, essays, and book reviews have appeared in numerous books and journals: *Adirondack Review*, *Anglican Theological Review*, *Tales for the Trail: Adventures in Air, Land, & Water* (Birch Brook), *Blueline Anthology* (Syracuse University Press), *Mystic River Review*, *Penwood Review*, and many other publications.

Pamela lives with her husband, Edward, in Oakland, California.

www.ingramcontent.com/pod-product-compliance
Lightning Source LLC
Chambersburg PA
CBHW070921160426
43193CB00011B/1552